Finding Heaven Now

Clem Suder

CLIMMER O SUDER
PUBLISHING

Finding Heaven Now

CLEM SUDER

Table of Contents

CHAPTER 1

Who Am I

As I have said in my first book A place for you, the end of days, the reason for all that I am writing this, is because I had a vision and was told to tell them what you see. The first book was about what is happening now and the visions I saw regarding that. It was obviously filled with dark images of what people have done to each other. It was the horrible images of past and present atrocities that have and will happen. It was given so that we could see the promise of things to come are just as true. It also points to the truth of what has been including the place emotionally and mentally you can go to which will preserve you no matter what others do. It is the place Jesus said, "I am going to prepare a place for you, and if I go, I will return and get you to take you there." After he was crucified, he did come back to show you the place is there and if you believe as he did it can protect you as well. It is because of the ongoing search by men to control others that most of the atrocities are committed. It is also because of misunderstanding value and true power that people seek by dividing all things so they can control them. What they fail to understand is that divided is always only part of the whole and never the entire whole, and therefore they seek to divide God himself, in order to feel they have control. Later in this book I will deal with this in significant detail. For now, it is just to begin to show you how all things fit and will come together which will allow you to be capable of having heaven even now. It was important to start at the point which is truly beyond people's control so you can see the truth in what was promised. I know that much that I am saying will be inconsistent with what people have sought and taught for years, but like the first book you can see it for yourself if you think about it and ask the father to help you understand. We know that physically there is strength in numbers, but spiritually all strength comes from within the individual and it is the spirit that is ongoing. The angels have been coming and going in human form from the beginning. This too I will deal with as we go along. As in all things the purpose, is paramount to properly understanding. It is this failure in understanding that has been the foundation of this existence. The understanding of the reason things operates the way they do will help you to see both the reality of what is there and the truth of what is promised, however unless you understand that it is how your goals coincide with the overall goal of creation that will allow both or put an end to your goals. How do we fail to understand? The bible tells us of how in the beginning in Eden that Adam and Eve were told that eating of the tree of knowledge of good and evil would make them as God themselves. From the standpoint of defining things for themselves it seems true. However, it ultimately proves pointless. You see it made them also alone without true purpose. Their purpose was divided from Gods purpose which is and always was to be continually greater. In fact, it is the basis for what we call nature it itself. It is the very definition of good which will always lead to more quality or quantity generally both. Again, without concern of what men think or do, if they work with it the outcome is good but if they don't, they suffer. You can if you understand this begin to get your first glimpse of heaven. You see the place we know as heaven is about the true value of the reason all of this was created. You see Jesus told a story about a father who was teaching his children something, so he called them into him and gave the each some value and told him he was going away for about a year. When he returned, he found one of his children working as a slave to another man and the second one when he went before the father went and dug up the value he had hidden and returned the original value to the father, the third said he had invested the value and it had grown significantly. Which one did the right thing? It is easy to point to the third and say because he raised the value of it, he did the right thing but now I challenge you to think from the viewpoint of the father, they all received a lesson which is what he intended so they all increased the value by learning to be like the father. I submit to you the story of this creation. Each will receive according to how they judge themselves. Either way the father will be greater. That is how heaven is greater for all and all increase because of their devotion to one cause being greater. This also identifies evil for what it is always less than and separate from the whole. That is clear in every way physically emotionally, and spiritually it is always less than what should have and could have been therefore it is not in heaven. This is truly sacrifice, the loss of value and strength. Good is mercy because it always increases. in my vision I went back to where I began which was in God and I got to see these things which became the reason for Eden and this world creation. It also required that in order to accomplish evil be used to promote the ultimate good. In other words, this portion which is less than be given to us so that we could learn to grow and ultimately raise the value of all. But typically, we want to blame someone else for what we chose to do.

But just as in Jesus' story ultimately the father did not lose value. Because we don't see the spiritual ordinarily it will be what you decide to believe that will either cause you to fail or to overcome. the joy or sorrow that we feel are the tangible physical results of our choice. If we experience the joy and all that is with it such as satisfaction, we can begin to see what we would have to describe as heaven. I hope you notice at no time in this story did I or Jesus refer to the use of force, that is one of the ways god deals with his children he does not need force, children resort to that to deal with each other and therefore, generally bring it upon themselves. It is odd how we fail to regularly see what Jesus told us about how we fear the one who can bring you the physical death but pay no attention to the one that can bring the second death or what we would think of as the spiritual death. In typical human fashion we need someone else to blame and say they forced me to, but it is only you who has the authority to give power to rule over you. And the father will give you what you empower. So, the bringer of the second death is you because it is a choice you made. Quit blaming God or anything else nothing has power over you unless you give it that power. That is the gift God gave you dominion in your world only not another person's world unless they give it to you.

You see it is what you believe that you allow to run your life. But even more since our father loves you so much, he gives you what you choose that makes you want to expect and demand that everyone believe as you do, and you never consider that even though they may not see things the way you do God gave them the same right to control their own world. In heaven you do not judge each other you constantly seek to help each other and raise each other up to allow both to have joy. If you want heaven you have to find ways to raise each other and share the joy with each other in order to truly understand, the joy only comes when you share with each other because you are independently aware of what you are sharing. I hope you can see now in all things it is what we find in each other and together with each other that will enable heaven to exist. So, we need to identify what is truly shared for all of Gods creation. The next thing that was in my vision was knowing our father who was and is and will be. to see and understand how we were in him in the beginning, and he is in us and we are one.

It is our blindness of the things that give true value that permits us to further the lie people teach, that it is what others seek that is the ultimate judge of value. It is the fear of death that gives this point of view power. Because you do not see that spiritually your energy is life, and it does not die because your body does. But because we have the authority to refuse to believe this lie, we have the ability to follow Jesus and not accept death only our body is subject to what we know as time space continuum. Or put another way our bodies portion of life. If you profess to be a Christian, you say you believe what Jesus said. If you do, then understand that the same place he emotionally and mentally prepared for you is there for you too. If you believe him, why do you fear death? It is because you believe he is apart from you and God is apart from you. The whole reason you believe that is that other men have determined that to be true even though Jesus said in the beginning I was in my father, my father is in me, and we are one, so I ask, who do you believe?

Having seen all the misery that has been and can be chosen I can truly tell you blessed is he who believes even though he does not see. As I went on my spiritual journey I went back through time and saw glimpses of the atrocities people committed to themselves and others by what they gave power to. I saw even things that were partially true twisted to end up being a source for the division of people. In the pacific I saw people hurling themselves to death on the rocks because of what they gave the power to rule over them. In Asia I saw the hordes who joined many tribes into one nation and the atrocities they committed in the process. In the middle east the death of Jesus because he challenged the authority of the church. In Greece the raise of democracy and the arts and sciences turn into rule by fear because they forced their religion on others. The raise of Rome who in the beginning sought to civilize and improve the ability to transport and raise the standard of living by providing martial protection with their armies. And how when they violated the rule of allowing people to worship as they please and began thinking of the emperor as a god their hundreds of year-old civilization was ravaged and destroyed. Europe who modified their concept of kingship to allow better representation of the individual. All of these had atrocities associated with them. To my final stop which was in heaven at least that is the impression I was given, the streets were not of gold in fact it seemed like a modern English village quaint with thatched roofs but clean and well-manicured. The biggest thing I noticed was the way people treated each other as though they were treating themselves. There was no judgement or assessment of each other only a willingness to help each other be successful in whatever they sought to do. They did not see each other's weakness because they were as each other's strength. They would absolutely recoil at any hint of division or judgement. To the point of making, it clears this was true value and it involved everyone there. This was as heavenly as I could imagine. It made me want to seek out the leadership to know more. What happened next in my journey was truly awesome. I was in a place that was majestic yet overwhelming in feeling. I am not one to willingly bend a knee to what I encounter but this was awesome. Yet, at the same time it was as though it were a father and a son just talking. I then understood that this was the father of all. Yet there was so much love and it seemed almost unconcerned about all that I was experiencing. I was overcome and asked why I got to see all of this? What was I supposed to do with this. I was told tell them what you see. At that point I said they won't believe me I can't tell them this they will kill me. Again, I was told tell them what you see. To which I said why me I am not a religious or political leader, I am just an old man in Georgia why will they hear me? At that time, I got to see what is coming yet, there would be so much misuse of power and authority that the people will seek relief and eventually take back the power they have given up. It is not in a martial way but in a manner of turning their back on any who propose division or misuse of others. The people begin to allow each other to receive what they have chosen and if it is to harm others, they harm the one who sought it. They rescinded the power others assumed they could not. The rule that they overthrew was based in fear and the time had come for people to stop living in fear and they understood that death of the body is not true death but a gateway to banding together with those who have already been and whose will be to increase the glory of god and all that is his not by any particular name but by the understanding truly of the I am.

The next chapter is more about this interaction and how and what I saw.

CHAPTER 2

The Answer Begins

I do not prejudge things I have learned to allow them to reveal themselves. And so it was in my vision, as a result I may have seemed to an observer not reverent enough, but I am not much on behaving as observer's would prefer because I know I am the only one who is accountable for what I do. So, if I'm going to assign any value to any situation, I try to make sure it is in keeping with what I believe. Perhaps it is that idiosyncrasy that caused it, but I think I was in awe. After spiritually being taken on such a journey and being overwhelmed by the input of so much information I was dumbfounded it also seemed that I reacted as I should have because it was truly like talking with a father who did not intend to harm me. Remember much of what I was receiving was perceived rather than conventionally heard. What I did know was that I was there for a reason, even though I was certainly not sure why me. Even as that realization struck me the answer did as well. Because he chose me. Not for anything I had done but despite all the weaknesses I had. It was like he was enjoying showing me what he was doing, after all I shook a world with a shepherd's son a carpenter in a time when getting information from one village to the next could take weeks. And he shook the world. The reason you are seeing this is because just as it was then it is time for what is to come now. The children cry out in their situation and even though they have allowed it to trouble them it is time they receive what they have empowered. You see the purpose of creation is the constant growth of me and all that I am in, which is everything. I am the living energy; all energy comes from me it is every form of energy. The people today look for the god particle because they think everything is limited as they are limited. They search microscopically for the particle and all they find are smaller particles. It will be like that for them to infinity, they search the heavens and the galaxies and find out they are constantly growing further apart. They search for newer understanding of energy all in hopes of furthering their own separate mastery over all things. Yet it is time they knew I am the alpha and the omega it starts and ends in me no matter how grand or how small. There are ways they can search and all it will end up is with a better understanding of me. Even the matter they seek to find the source of is from me the constant interaction of the various forms of energy have a biproduct that they work with you know it as matter. Even then you know a very small amount because of the surrounding conditions in which they are working which you call time because it does not change but it changes what is in it. Al of this was accomplished and more because I always increase, I always get greater in every way. The matter you call you is the temple of the living energy that I have given you. Without that portion your body would not function. Before you were the energy that is your soul was in me and I give it to you, so we are one. The form of energy that is your will is from me as well but because for it to grow it must be shared with another who possesses it as well it must be a choice you make to share it with whom you will. If it is in keeping with my will which is the increase of all it can lead to greater if it is not going to function in a way that allows the continued growth of all that is me, it will be ended. The purpose of this creation was to give you the ability as part of me to increase, which is why if you do the things that allow growth you get more but if you divide and waste what you have been given you suffer. It is the way things are ordered men have gotten so bad at trying to erase the consequence for doing bad that they are speeding up what will cause their own destruction. This is the reason Jesus told you I require mercy I do not require sacrifice. This describes the difference.

When the world was at the point that it could take years to get a message of division from one place to another intervention on a smaller scale was enough. But now you seek weapons that will destroy all, and it takes seconds to foment hate and distrust around the globe and men have the audacity to seek to conquer galaxies the intervention will be according to what you seek. I know you say you have no control over the world which is why Jesus' message of facing even crucifixion in order to show you that death as you know it is not the end but the beginning for those who choose it was required when it was. So too it is not who I send but the message they deliver that is important. You see everyone must die the first death, but they choose for themselves the second by separating themselves from all. So many think that because God allows people to get the results of what they choose it is too hard. The reality is since the first death is not the end unlike people who remove the consequences for each other and their children on the small things then fail to understand why their children choose things that have much harder consequences. God is allowing us to learn on the small things. It is we who choose the worst things. Just as in the time of Sodom and Gomorrah everyone was killed, and people think it cruel because surely everyone was not guilty since they allowed those who allowed those things, they were guilty. That may seem harsh, but it is reality. So, if you look at what is happening in the world around you today, you see the mounting cries of the people. Because he gave this time and place to us, he wants us to care for each other. That does not mean do for each other but help everyone who is helping themselves. By doing for them they do not participate in the joy of overcoming.

All that is created is by the energy that is the constant of God we cannot conceive of it let alone try to contain it in a name. yet because we are on with in it, we think we can separate ourselves from it because of the specific energy that is will. The energy that is all energy is of and is God. It is in all that was created and is there is so much more that we don't know about energy, yet we presume to be apart from it as we discover more like space is not devoid it is full of energy, and it is not stagnate but continually expanding. There are other forms of energy we have no concept of but as we further seek to divide so we can define we think our definition gives it the power. Just as the power of God is in us it is in all that he created and if it functions for the increase of all it will not trigger the consequences of failure. It is not limited by space and time it can assume different forms it can appear as physical form but is not limited to time space. It is truly extradimensional in its nature. We are connected yet isolated we do not understand it because we cannot limit it. We think of energy in a sense of not having a reasoning force but when you put the force of reasoning with it truly become unfathomable. So, you see this sounds so incredible, yet it is. It comes down to how can we see from the perspective of what leads to more. If we begin to see things from that perspective much of what has been and what is coming are explained. Heaven as a result of a place that creates a certain type of energy that fueled the growth of all is a logical conclusion. In order to have that here every individual must choose it to be in it. Those who choose to be apart from it literally condemn themselves to the inability to interact and raise the true value of existence. Is it any wonder that the ancients referred to it as sleeping.

As we have seen in this chapter the explanation of Jesus statement that he was one with God does not replace the God who is. Because they could not comprehend much of what he said and did from a cultural perspective they did what people do which is set him apart from all, he was proving just the opposite we are one. In order to exist in and have heaven you cannot separate yourself from all the prophets or from God. Because the prophet's messages were Gods messages to us, and them like all are in him for him and with him. It is this fact that caused many years of failing to write these books and get them out there. If they killed such as these, why would they hesitate to kill an old man from Georgia. It really took a long time to understand enough to do this. I was so proud of myself for overcoming my fear, but it turns out everything has a time, and it is as it should be. it is not my choice to choose the time. I have to say since so many define God by so many names, I was afraid of people being upset because I did not use their definition as God, but he immediately corrected me there. No name can contain him. So, what I can tell them is true just as his energy is in all things so is he your definition is yours if it does not divide or do evil by judging someone else only you will be accountable for it.

One of the things that I was afraid of is that people would say because I had this vision it set me apart. I want them to know it was Gods choice not mine and he does not like people asking him to jump through hoops to prove to them anything. I saw what he intended I see, and he told me to tell what I saw, if killing me will make you feel better ok. But it won't change what is to be.

I hope each one will ask our father themselves to show them the truth in all that I have said. But I am afraid few will take the time or even listen for the answer. Many will take it to their church and ask them not realizing they are doing what I and Jesus told them not too, when they do that, they put the word of men between them and God. I hope they would read their scriptures again because no man has a greater understanding than God himself. I am not telling you what I heard from someone else's mouth I am telling you what I saw. I am also pointing out what it says in the bible throughout the bible heaven will be here on earth. If you believe and know you can really only control your own life, why do you wait, live like you are there now. This is wisdom, the form of energy we call will as all energy of God has always been, t is when this energy is expressed in what we know as time that remarkable things can happen. It is the fashion that was created for you to have your portion. It is the boundary of things as you know them. It is the border of your portion so when there is a black hole the energy that is in this dimension which always seeks to be greater rushes into the new void which is also of energy but of a different nature due to its parameters. This we call dimensions they actually coexist but are working under separate parameters. So, while both exist at the same time only the ones that can manifest in your parameter becomes visual, or fully capable of interaction. Again, the energy was there first but the energy of will was operating under other interactions with the other forms of energy. So, you see God was already there we are trying to expand our dimension to be more. It is time you can understand more because the borders are about to change which will allow time separation to be suspended which will allow what has been to interact with what is. In other words, the dead will be again interacting more actively than ever. You could say the dead will rise. But it is not for your purpose it is for the purpose and will of God. Sounds kind of crazy but if you think of it you deal with a form of it every day of your life when the energy of the individual interacts with the matter and concepts of those who came before you have what your world is today. However, as you can see the world under poor or ignorant guidance will always lead to suffering and death not because God chose it but, because you allowed it. Heaven does not have your parameters and limitations so unless you are capable of not seeking those limitations you will not be in heaven. As in all things you are part of not the whole of the father and you have gifts to accomplish his goals if you use them, you will receive more than you can even imagine.

CHAPTER 3

What Was, And Is To Be

The first days of earth were given to those who had chosen the knowledge of good and evil. They were filled with new sensations that they never really needed or have in heaven. The main over all feeling was that of being isolated. It was so alien that it made them seek to isolate themselves further. So much so that when our father came near, he knew they had separated themselves. The bible says they realized they were naked, since naked had not even known then, it is the first reference to sex. As a result of that association sex became entangled with people's perception of the original sin. Because of the immediate association of sex with being separate everyone new that sex and the feeling assigned to it could make the other person experience shame. It became one of the primary control mechanisms that people used to control one another. It was a personal display of weakness that no other creature demonstrated. What it taught them was that while you could not directly control one another's feelings in a natural state, you could have your feelings manipulated. The initial concept of society relied on this to control conduct in the group. For this to work you had to convince the individual the group new more than the individual about feelings. If this manipulation worked how about the value of what something means or should mean? This is the belief that society relied on to establish economic and monetary scales how much your feeling should be worth. The fact that God gave the individual the right to determine what they would feel about and why by doing this he gave you dominion of your own world only. In heaven the individual was never disconnected from the whole in this world that truth they thought they could change. The reason for that goes back to Lucifer telling them that the knowledge would make you feel like God, what he did not tell you is that because God gave you the right to choose, others can also choose what they want. Therefore, people thought of themselves as God and that meant what was important to them should be important to all. In order to get what they wanted they had to control what others felt. The way to do this has all to do with, how and what people decide what they will feel about and why. This is possible by fear and force. Either to convince them that someone ese knows better than you or killing those who chose something else.as a result when someone talked abOut God their response was to kill those who did not understand him the same way they did. That is why in the Old Testament and many of the oldest scriptures the people were supposedly told to kill everyone and everything. This type of doctrine furthered the division and isolation of individuals and groups as well. They justified this by saying you would receive the worth of those people you had removed. Again, the concept of worth being and maintained by something else besides yourself. Because it works to a point more and more people bought into the concept. It continued again and again and gradually expanding the depth of control others exercise over each other it continues to this day and is a repetitive process. The fact that in groups your ability to defend yourself and others increases is the truth they used to produce the fear of being unable to defend yourself or accepting the right for society to determine what and how much you should feel. It is the kernel of truth in their lie. That is why it is demonstrated repeatedly the miraculous exceptions. To the point that people gave their sons and daughters to be killed in the attempt to give the leadership of their social group's desires. It continues today and it continues to remove true value from your lives, it increases still the isolation. It is this underlying lie that has brought the world to the brink of self-destruction. The fact that God gave the feelings of good when you are involved sexually physical nerve cause you to feel good. But to society they had to make you overcome those feelings and allow them to tell you what you should feel. That is, it becomes important to enforce their concept. The reality of the fact that love does not operate by property right laws. Makes this control evidently false without threat to enforce the property law aspects, because this is in reality a lie we have deteriorated as a society. Up to and practically through the destruction of the nuclear family. So, you see the many lies we give authority over our lives by allowing the concept that others know more or have the power to establish our feelings, do not change the fact that you have control only of your own feelings and life.

I hope you will take the time to see how the prophets tried to tell you and show you the same thing. And in seeing what they said instead of what someone else said about them or said they said you can find the truth. When you find the truth no matter what time in history or whatever situation you look at it never changes, the truth does not change. There are many prophets from different religious back grounds, but the truth does not change, so you need to see that they are just as relevant today as they were in their time. This understanding will help you to see what was said will happen if you seek the truth know that while the things they talked about or tried to explain was and is contained in understanding. That is why most people can't even describe what heaven should be like. It is also the reason that society is being torn apart by people who promote lies. Statements about someone hurting your feelings, when you obviously didn't care about theirs. Promoting the policies that have only one end in destruction giving authority to lies as though they were truth. I will talk a great deal about one prophet in particular, Jesus, because he told you the truth in a way that others had to hide because they did not see or understand what he was telling them. Therefore, he is the messiah because he told the truth. We talk about how he died for us, but he talked about how he lived for them. People chose to deify him separately even though he never said to. He said to deify our father who is in all. he said in the beginning I was in my father; my father is in me, we are one. This is what the lie cannot allow because it takes away the authority, they try to convince you they have over you. Again, the doctrine of men is to be apart from God. Because they can demand that what they say is the truth. All is contained it is when you try to concentrate on the parts without trying to improve all you throw away what you don't include.

People would say what they do not understand is not real, and they can't understand the things Jesus said. I am going to point out to you that Jesus told his followers that because of him father against son mother against daughter, brother against brother. Because he saw what was going to come. He saw what they could not see. The churches and Christian religion like all religion is controlled by men and teaches what men want to hear because of their perceived economic and power structure again based on what they could control as value. He told them what was going to happen, in fact it went like this, "who do people say I am? you think I came to give you peace I have given you a sword. It was his vision of the thousands of tears about to happen around the context and failure to understand we are one. Again, it is about power men want to be the ones who say who will have power. It is important that you understand this because it reinforces the prediction of a thousand years before Jesus. This prophecy also talked of two witness and what was to be. the first part was done with Jesus, so I would say the second part is as assured to come as well. In fact, many have taken the liberty to say how that comes to be. they talk of armies from heaven lead by Jesus to destroy those who stood against the church's teachings. Even though he refused to condemn even the ones who hung him. They have him coming back to judge us. After all of the teaching he did over not judging others, they cast him as a judge. At best they cast him as a defense attorney. Who paid so we could miss behave. They say that all you must do is say his name, when he said in the end many will come to me saying" lord, lord." And "I will say to them why do you call me lord when you do not do what I said." You must try to be as he is and as he was. It is not worth nothing it is to discover the true father. All the things I talk about here is what he said. We watch movies and think of people who stood for what they believed even up to death. We think of them as heroes, as long as they lost their lives in what we consider at the time

16

valuable. It is easiest when it is society that supports this. However, today religions and truth are ridiculed. All form the constant process of reducing the only true value with the value of society, or I should say the mob.

It is the entire process of how you decide value or worth that is the question. They want to maintain value as a mysterious quality that only they can decide. If it be in spiritual or material, it is theirs to control. This has caused millions of people to die. They rely on you teaching your children that they know better. As a result, your sons and daughters die at someone else request. Then they wonder why it only leads to more atrocities. Still, they try to ask it a moral question because they don't think you can supply truth or question them with fact. Unfortunately, people still offer their sons and daughters lives to people who believe they are entitled to demand the death of our children. They don't think they are one of the people they think they are better than the people and despite the deaths we allow it. There are times when we are and should be committed to helping protect our neighbors, if they ask for and try to defend themselves. It should not be done on a limited basis because our children's lives are at stake. To begin with the concept of killing them all is the way war should be conducted. That way people will stop playing games with life. It should horrify all who seek to enter war. That is the way it will stop. We are one and the only way to be one is to live as one. Do not judge each other but hold each accountable to how they judge themselves by what they say and do. No political figure should be reelected if they are responsible for the death of our children by failing to provide the proper support to those they send in harm's way. To enter a war zone in less than full force is to play with war and all it does is keep the failed leadership in charge. If you commit to help do all you can to protect and help or your commitment means nothing. I know people will react in horror at such a suggestion but World War three will happen as a result of the failure of people to understand true value and allowing the loss of all the freedoms God gave you. It will just seem to take longer until one side or the other uses weapons of mass destruction. I know what is coming and that is yet to be told what I have talked about to this time has and is happening now.

Destroy this temple and I will rebuild it in three days. That is what Jesus told the Jewish church leadership. It sounds unbelievable today, just as it did then. What do you think your reaction to that would be if a trial was covered on tv today and the defendant said such a thing? Is there any wonder why you say Jesus next return will be at the head of an army? Have you ever considered that God hid Jesus from Herod in spite of the prophets telling him what was going to happen, until he had done what he was sent to do. Are you so convinced that God wants to kill you that the only saving grace is a war? and what do you think the ground rules for such a war only people from a certain portion of a certain religion are left alive and only the dead of that religion will be raised? Or do they do as the Old Testament says and kill them all? Or is it liking the scriptures say and the second witness just like the first is killed and then raised in three days. I know it says that there will be an army from heaven and the dead will be raised to join that army, but consider what God would feel with the destruction of so many of his children? More importantly how would God grow from that? I am suggesting that you will think about what you have been taught and how you have given it the power over you. Because that is how you will be judged by yourself. Are you free as Jesus was? Can you hang on the cross based on what your church taught you? If you did, could you forgive those who hung you, or even remember they were just doing their job? Could you hang there and talk to God? Would you have even gone knowing what was about to happen? As I have told you from his own words and mouth he knew. I know there have been other prophets that talked about what has been and even what will be in many different religions even those that have been to heaven to see God. How many came back telling you God wants you all to die? Or to go out and kill anyone who does not agree with you? If they did, they would not be around long. As clearly, I have stated their followers may say that they did but that is not in any way serving anyone or God. I have told you to check for yourself ask our father he wants to hear from you if you call yourself a Christian do as he told you and even from the cross talk to the father. if you are not a Christian or you do not know have the guts to talk to God as your father and see how he answers you it may take some getting used too we don't even do a good job of listening to each other. I am sorry if you don't feel you can talk to God or if you feel others have to, or should talk to him for you. You might struggle thinking what language trust me just like this vision I am writing to you about no language necessary.

I guess as I have been trying to show you the past and the present are tied together so is the future, so I need to start with now. I hope you will forgive me it has been over a year since I sat down and listened to any news coverage for more time than it takes to change the channel or turn it off. I rely on understanding why and what will happen. It is not that difficult if you understand true value and the means men use to create the value, they want you to believe. The reason I have done this is the same understanding what others say are indications of how they judge themselves, since the prevailing sentiment is to allow others to dictate to you what they want you to believe. In short, the news used to just be reported and it was allowed to judge itself by the results of what it created. People were free to decide for themselves what it represents. Today the news is a tirade of politically motivated policy. And it is spun for that effect. It is accomplished again by value, or social value which is money. Again, the reporters sell their integrity for political approval. This lack of standing for what you believe is fueling the loss of social value. It is further reinforcing the fear to stand up for your belief. It used to be you might have suffered some verbal insult and harm, today it could easily be physical harm. If they can brazenly do this in front of the entire public and suffer no consequences, think Sodom and Gomorrah, they can certainly be bought. This is an indicator of how far the progression of loss of true value has advanced. It is also an indicator of the state of the people that they would allow it to go this far. Again, the loss of faith which can be demonstrated is the result of the failure of religions to demonstrate the relevant truth. Teaching a partial truth is just setting it up for total rejection. That is why today so many say that God is a concept that is not real. Again, the result of not being able to point to the causative failures in a world that has advanced to the point what you say now can be on the other side of the earth in seconds. when most of the scriptures were written it may have taken years or decades to get out of the continent they were written on. With the increase of the speed of communication so also the loss of true value because people do not understand the nature of true value which is what enables others to replace what you value with what they value, and use it to belittle and reduce your understanding, but all that really happens is that you feel depressed and less than what you should have felt which is empowered. It your willingness to accept what others say in place of what you see is that loss of value that they rely on because you feel the loss but do not understand it, they tell you your faith is misplaced. Because you accepted their words over your feelings your faith is misplaced. They want to talk about me when me is we, you lose the ability to raise the joy and value of life with everyone you cut out of your life, and to cut someone out because someone else told you too without seeing with your own eyes, and directly from that person prevents you from finding ways to find we, and the me is really the society rather than you. It really is summed up in some simple old-time wisdom, if someone tells you to jump off a cliff would you, do it? Is just as true if you accept someone else's statement that God does not exist. Their understanding of God is faulty. They envision themselves as God and want to demand that everything is as they say. Instead of true value which is their feelings that only them can feel. You see God himself gave you the authority to decide what and how much you will feel is yours. In that way you establish what you value. If you understand that then you understand true individual value. It is reinforced by what is real. And when you find someone who genuinely feels as you do those feelings are magnified and intensified, it is the only true way to increase the value of your feelings and it is this process to raise the joy of living that is the reason you were given this time and place. Raising the value of creation is what it was created for. It always leads to more it is good. What is evil loses value always.as simple as it is it is the one knowledge that empowers creation itself. It is the one teaching that Jesus kept trying to make clear to you, it is this that he gave to you because of this you can truly see why he is the savior. Yet all those around sought to turn his words to what they felt and since people seek what they knew death became the gift he gave not the freedom of value. Look at the world around you. There are people who say there is no god. And it is being given authority socially. Socialism which is all about supposedly the distribution of value according to someone else scale. A political system that can only work by the stealing of the individuals value and because of that fault it contains its own destruction. Which is why it can never succeed. While people cannot define things, they deny the existence of them. People seek lies as though they are the truth.

There are wars and rumors of wars there are smart disease and pandemics. It seems I have heard that before, OH yes, it is in the bible and even though this particular thing was written about three thousand years ago it has to be a modern hoax according to new stream thinking.

Let us consider some of the other social things going on now in the world. Racism, it is unfortunate that it ever existed, but it has existed as long as men have been in any social form. The difference is that today we hold the grandchildren accountable for what their grandparents did. It doesn't matter that in most cases the ones that sold others into slavery were the same race and there are and have been probably slaves of every race and ethnicity, but we will select one race to blame for this. We won't hold those grandchildren of the ones who sold their brethren into slavery or the ones of the same race that bought their brethren and sold them to another race. We really don't have accurate figures but we still have places in the world white, Latino, Asian and blacks are still enslaved but we want to hold the people of one of the countries that will not allow slavery responsible for the system. We don't consider the fact that for socialism to come to power in China the death of forty million people, in the Soviet Union twenty million people disappeared, but there is no injustice according to the social mainstream because they are socialist. The fact that system can only exist as long as it has people to steal from and an elite portion of people to decide who gets what. It seems while they seek and promote this system as a social goal in spite of the facts that until a country that has the military force, and the concentration of force to have dissenters disappear into it is a stylish lie that people are not, protesting. So amazing how that someone thousands of years ago would see that coming. By the way all those things were written about the end of the world as we know it. Or the end of days. How they could have seen all of this is impossible and it must be a plot. The truth is being denied daily. So, you see the future is also rooted in the past what I have said are what Jesus said I have detailed why and how you can see for yourself. They point out how and why all of this is logical and can be apparent for you. It has all been before you for thousands of years, yet it has not been taught. A different way of seeing things or a new perspective. Yet it requires all that has happened in order to see it. Yet they knew it was coming thousands of years ago. It is what is happening today without stretching or trying to make what was said fit what is going on. This is important to see in order to see what is still to come. As crazy as it may sound it is how exact the match between what was said and what is. I know that people have been trying for years to make what has been foretold to the world they live in. like most things if you think you must manipulate things to make them fit it is probably not true. What I have told you to this point is something that you can check and see for yourself. What I am about to tell you. Is something that I hope you will understand and see for yourself. In order to see and know what is in the future you must see what has been, which is what I have told in this book. As well as other people telling the same story when there is no way to collaborate. What you choose to believe must come from within. People are so used to thinking someone can force someone else to see, but I promise you this if you think God will force you or anyone to change to be in heaven you will never see heaven. No force is any part of heaven and that is also what is going to happen here. Whether you believe what I will say here or not does not change the truth of what will be. everyone wants to know the hour and minute, yet as long as they worry about time, they will never see heaven, it is a choice not forced. The whole point of this book is finding and raising the value of life to be in heaven that is how you and everyone who will be there to choose and live. If you think anyone needs changed by an outside source, you or they will not be in heaven. It is almost impossible for people who claim to have faith to think that heaven can occur on earth yet that is also told what is coming. How much faith do you have, how limited by your judgement are you?

I ask you to consider the state of the world in complete detail, what do you think the world values? What do you think the people have faith in? how do you think most people expect the end of the world as we know it.

How many people seem open to understanding anything given that most people do a terrible job of listening to themselves or to each other. So how many do you think are willing to listen to what so many think does not exist?

You may not like it or agree with it but what you are about to hear will happen. You may not recognize the transition in the seemingly small steps, but they will occur rapidly. Because so many are expecting intervention, they may not see the change in the individual but that is where the change will be. because and connected to the judgement day. It has begun and people will judge themselves. What I will tell you is how it can affect or protect you. It is not my purpose to tell you what has already been established will happen the end of days as you know them with people fighting over things that are not value will come to an end brought on by their greed and wish to keep their eyes closed. They will be provided with whatever it takes to open their eyes by their fellow man's greed and demand for what they cannot have. It is like walking into a blackened room and someone turns the light on. Nothing changed but you see what is before you. So it will be the question is will you wait too long to stop it without massive loss of life. I hope so but I doubt you have the strength it will take to turn your back and refuse to support or be a part of it and that will just cost more lives, mostly your children's.

CHAPTER 4

Power and Energy

As I have told you in my vision, I saw the past I also glimpsed the future. I will not tell you specifics of what I saw only the reasons that they will happen. Just as in the past there are choices you all must make and in order to find the place of absolute surety and comfort you must be so committed to what you choose that fear has no foot hold. Lt is the reason that the first book was apart from this, and the time required it. As in all things you look to another to show you your reality and think what they see will automatically lock you into a course of action. The fact is you and only you have the authority to give what you will, power over you. As I go forward in this book, I will try to expose some of the partial truths that people have clung to for years thinking that what they perceive must be what everyone should see. The difference of what I have written and will write is I tell you to check it for yourself, and you decide. Each person perceives what they choose, and it is only when they choose to allow what others say to have power over them that the understanding has any power. And because of the partial truth that there is strength in numbers of people you allow things power over themselves until it becomes so painful, they can no longer accept it. That has always been the case and there are people who live to exercise this over other to get what they want even though it is not good for the whole. That is part of the basics of what you were meant to be, a blessing to each other. Because of the energy of will in your life you either understand and support what is good for all or you suffer the loss of the value and joy you could have been able to receive. It is one of the automatic features of true nature that supports the constant growth of our creator. Even though you may not see or understand it, this was designed to reward those who serve to increase the joy of living for all, or to take away the joy of some thinking, it will be overshadowed by the joy they receive by accomplishing their individual goals. The cost of those types of misguiding have grown much higher I point out the last two world wars and the continued loss of peace and security since. It is this loss of peace and security that has and will be the fueling mechanism for those things that are and are about to happen.

You see it is the partial truth that value is in the definition and control of others that in the end will destroy all who hold to that. We do that by the approximation of value we call money. It is worth what others convince you it is worth, however if you find someone who needs what you are gifted with the ability to do, and they produce something their gifts give them a unique ability to produce you can barter. Again, it requires the agreement of both parties of the value of the objects in the deal. So, the more personal the deal the less encroachment by others will be effective. Which is why that system is not encouraged, it is difficult at best to tax. Because of your audacity to use a method that cannot be taxed well you will face punitive measures mostly vague but still consequential. The reason it is a partial truth is that if you do not agree to allow others to set your value you will be punished by society as opposed to the natural consequences. You see nature does not answer to our time parameter so for many it is not fast enough or for that matter according to them harsh enough. The reality that it exists to guide people to decisions that will be the best for all, and it does not willingly seek the destruction of individuals is not sufficient because it does not immediately support their goals. So, nature will slowly work to cause you to change your understanding and if you will not it will destroy you. That is what nature was designed to enforce, the increase of all, not the decrease. If we do not give it the regard it should have it will do whatever It takes to correct what we have done. Many of the things we see today are the result of that change to enforce truth. It is also why the bible continually speaks of how in the end times there will be draught, and floods and famine as well as plagues we could call pandemic. So, people want to think of these things as the rage of God while in fact it is just the opposite the natural process to cause the growth of all through the elimination of those who support the loss of so much. Remember what I told you about the power of will, it must be properly guided in the respect to the growth of ALL that is going to avoid the consequence of nature itself. you see this is the natural progression of the half-truths people have taught and support because they think it gives power to them over others, it is true there are consequences but not because of alienation to our thinking. The consequences are the result of true origin and purpose this was created for it has nothing to do with emotion it is about value and getting greater. It is the purpose of creation that can help us understand the nature of creation, but we must be able to dispassionately allow the process of things judging themselves to be able to accurately comprehend the process of creation. Since people think they are entitled and in fact exist to judge others they violate each other in ways that will feed and cause further judgement because they think their understanding is the only truth there can be. they do so in ignorance. True judgement requires the complete understanding of what and why anything happens. If you know the truth that God gave everyone the right to judge only themselves because they are the only ones who can know what and why they did what they did. So, your judgement of them is no longer a natural progression. And therefore, will only engender feelings in those who choose to allow it. It is this pursuit of this idea that you have the right to judge others that causes so much misery. And it will continue to cause misery until you reserve your judgement to yourself since only you can honestly answer the questions of what and why you and only you did anything. Judging others will always cause loss. And you need to understand that just that action is opposed to the purpose nature itself exists, it will cause consequences, you won't even connect the two because you do not truly understand the creation or the purpose of creation and the true function of nature itself.

So, you can begin to glimpse how half-truths and misunderstanding has led to such misery. You could say it begins with the concept god created this place and this portion for the purpose of punishing us. The concept of forcing desired action, it is what people must use but God does not need to force anything. The ultimate purpose of the creation of the nature of creation was to without passion enforce the purpose of all of creation, the growth of all. It is the energy and power of will that is required in judgement. When you express your will, you are setting yourself up for failure if you do not remember that God gave everyone the right to choose what they will give the power of will to what they feel they must. If you do not allow the right to everyone to choose what they will you are saying that God made a mistake, God does not make mistakes we do. I often think as I watch what others say and do how many mistakes do they think the creator of all made? Some will look at what I say and think energy does not have form, to them I would suggest, go out into a hurricane and feel the form energy can create. Just like us a hurricane is the result of the interaction of many different forms of energy. It does not possess the energy of will. We fail to understand the significance of this form of energy because it is the form that gave us dominion in our world. It is so important that Jesus told the Sanhedrin destroy this temple and I will rebuild it in three days, and he did it. Consequentially it can be understood that the energy of will is so strong it literally overcomes the energy of life itself. It is the form of energy God gave to everyone, but society maintains it comes from them. This failure is one of the ways societies wants to determine for the individual their value system. It is the thing that people must control in order to control each other. It is unfortunate that they think any deviation from their chosen path is going to lead to destruction in fact if they reinforced the reality that it is the individual the power to increase all they would remove the allure of criminal pursuit. It may take more time but nature itself will enforce that it is the increase of all that is the purpose of creation. If you choose to do otherwise eventually you will pay the price. Even society will fail the more they get into removing the value of the individual. Unfortunately, it ends up coming in the form of destruction of the leaders of that social structure. Even in democracy if you allow the leadership to destroy the value of the individual you support the reduction of value it will inevitably cause your own destruction. This is the condition of the world today; it exists because society presumes to have to establish the value of the individual rather than realizing it is the failure of the society to reinforce the gift God gave only the individual to establish true value. It will always result in the loss of value and eventually on a scale that will cause revolt. The leadership because they have lost touch with the individuals, they are supposed to govern lose the respect for them and feel they have power of force to make them fall in line. It is truly unfortunate that people cannot see or hear the feelings of those around them because the delay is what feeds the destruction. I know many of you will say that this is deep thinking, it is only observing the truth. If you look at every situation for how it helps everyone, and if there are any that will be harmed by your course of action, all you have done is delayed the reaction and usually the delay will make the repercussions more expensive.

We are ready to face the reality that God created this place to give each of us the ability to judge ourselves. This is done by what we say and do. If you elect leadership that believes socialism the forced equalization of everyone's worth, you support stealing from someone who earned the value to give it to someone who cannot appreciate the value they receive which automatically throws that value away. This brings us to understanding one of the misunderstood stories in the bible, the raising of the dead. Remember how Jesus told the Sanhedrin if they destroyed this temple, he would rebuild it in three days. I told you it was the result of will. His will being in concert with the fathers, so it was the fathers will not just his will. This will become the foundation of the raising of the dead. It is not because it is the will of one man it is the will of the creator and source of all energy. Remember at the time most of society would not have cared what happened to Jesus. So, as I go forward, I want you to remember that outside of the prophets who foretold what would happen most people knew very little about it and had you told them this story even though they existed at the same time they would have thought you were crazy. That and the fact that as Jesus said because of him, mother against daughter, father against son, brother against brother, he brought a sword. Pretty odd for someone to put themselves on that important level. Then to have the story not go away but eventually be worldwide should be sufficient when people question the accuracy of what transpired. Think of the time and how splintered societies were at that time it should make you marvel at how the story grew without divine intervention. For all of those who question if any of it were true, I hope they will be realistic enough to know that while today he seems so presentable at that time, he was unknown. A small-town story in a time without social media to present it to everyone. How many small-town stories do you know even with the modern forms of communication are world known today? We get outraged over the deaths in traffic accidents which happens by the hundreds how many would notice the death of one? Remember at that time the Romans literally lined the major roads with the crucified. So, what would cause this one to be so unforgettable. I will be the first to say much of what the churches teach today should be questioned because they teach what others say about him rather than his own words. Everything I have written in this book and the previous book is one hundred percent based on what he said and how that is in keeping with the will of our father. I was fortunate to have had the vision that put all of this in the perfect perspective. That I could understand. But I believe it was to put this vision in writing before the world so you can decide for yourself. So, many want miracles in order to believe if what I have pointed out about a small-town story becoming one of the major talking points of the world two thousand years later, if that's not a true miracle you won't see what you would believe anyway. The other thing that makes me say that is you want miracles to support this book. I am sorry I will not jump through hoops for your approval, and neither should the creator of all. I do not need to judge you since you have just judged yourself. That is how true judgement works.

What is to come is the result of your giving away the gifts god gave you, which is the energy of will, you gave it to society. Because you have chosen this you will receive what society gives you or takes from you. This will cause more shortages and outages because people don't have to work for themselves and are punished if they do. Nothing maintains sufficient value to cover the actual cost of not punishing and keeping others in line. This initial cessation of material will eventually lead to the realization that what has been said is real. That will cause people to realize heaven can and will be here, not because someone else said it because they are aware it is only the individual that can truly experience it since society does not dictate it. A final realization that our father loves ALL of us and makes us accountable for how we judge ourselves. This realization will cause individual to not interact or support people who do anything that divides and separates Gods children.

There are people who would rather see the destruction of all mankind then to allow others to choose the freedom that God gave us individually the right to decide what we will value, because it removes their ability to dictate to us. So real is this concern that everyone wants to know about the end of time. I cannot tell you what does not exist there is no end to what god has made. There is an end of days for each of us. Time will continue as a portion God has given to us. Even if the leadership seeks to destroy all of mankind they will not succeed. There will be survivors. And they will re-populate. Just like controlling nature we cannot do it. We never will, but it will always support and enable the growth that is the will of God. It is up to the people who choose leadership that seeks to divide and support division of the people within their society. The churches who do not teach the failure of judgement. They support the continuing division of the children of God because they have the audacity to choose to think the church does not know all and because the church feels it can judge the children of God obviously the members must have that authorization. They call themselves Christian and yet do the one thing he told them repeatedly not to do. Is it any wonder why he told his followers in the end many will come to me saying lord, lord, and I will say to them, why do you call me lord when you do not do what I say? I don't know you. I am sorry to those judgmental people and churches I don't know you either. You call Jesus the Messiah the savior of the world, I hope you can see now what he is saving themselves from mankind. We demand payment and do not think the increase of God is payment enough for us. But it is the reason and driving force of creation itself. God always gets greater and since we can do things that reduce ourselves, we think God must be apart from us. What Jesus told us ss that God is not apart from us, but we are in him, and he is with us. He told us if we don't judge by our standards which is the increase of the individual but by the father's standard which is the increase of all including the individual. Because we demand payment of blood, we say that is what he did. In fact, we say you will be saved just knowing his name, the reality of the fact you need to understand what and why he said what he did is something the church teaches is not important. Believe in what he knew for himself you don't need to know it yourself. Why do you call me lord when you do not what I said?

He taught us that before we were we were in the father and while we are the father is in us and we are one. If you believe what he said you are saved from the one who would divide all of gods creation, mankind. That is who you are saved from so why do you still give society the power to rule over you? It is right to help each other overcome the obstacles in their lives because that helps the growth of all. That is the purpose of creation, it is the fathers will, if you do that life gets better and more rewarding for all. That is the mark God has set for each of us. If we hit this mark, we receive the benefits of better more rewarding life. When we fail to hit this mark we sin, that is we missed the mark. In the bible when it talks about the sons of Israel it talks of one of the tribes who were great archers and never sinned or missed the mark. But as usual we want to impose our judgement over the fact. Men seek ways and reasons to punish each other rather than ways to grace each other. The difference with grace is that we know that we make mistakes and yet unless it was intentional it will not engender a natural response.

It is this understanding that will raise the dead, it is mercy that requires they who gave their lives for the increase of all through the increase of our father, not by human names which we use to divide understanding but the increase of one who cannot be contained in a name. the father of all creation not just the ones we know and think he can. The increase requires each individual increase in the joy and reward of their feeling. This can only happen when both parties understand and feel the same thing when they share that feeling the increase in joy and reward is what mercy is. This is how the energy of life is increased. This is what people must learn to find in every moment of every day in order to experience heaven. All of this was foretold thousands of years ago. In the next chapters I will show alternative ways this could happen.

CHAPTER 5

Deliver Me

As I have said previously it is told several times in the bible some of the things that will happen in the end of days. Many people think of that as the end of time and that is because they cannot conceive of life existing in any other form than what they can accept. The bible itself is something that corrects that error. It spans thousands of years and still has a cohesive story that seems to work without concern to what we say or do. Consequently, there is much consternation about what real can be. this is due to our uncertainty of understanding what real is. we try to rely on each other's experiences to determine confirmation of what we should believe. It is this misunderstood need that is played on by people to establish their own desire. Part of the reason for all this consternation is the fact that words have different meaning to those who use them. It is safe to say that words used in conversation two thousand years ago are not likely to have the same meaning today. Simply because our understanding is so much broader today. Still there are those who maintain the way they understand the words used must be the correct understanding of what they were supposed to mean when they were used. For instance, the word heavens definition is subject to perspective, such as the skies, or the universe, or a spiritual place that is not seen. This is just an example of the variety of meanings that can be assumed for each word used. Because they were used thousands of years ago in an area that had several different dialects some of which are not even spoken anymore, we must rely on what we think the intent was. As I have said I am not here to tell you what you should believe, but rather present alternative perspectives I received as a result of my vision. I will try to define those things I can see right away that may cause concern hoping you will see as I did.

In the previous chapters I have begun to deal with some of the most momentous events such as the raising of the dead. Perhaps one way this could be explained is the power of will of those who were here before us. Our ancestors' thoughts and desires that have created the beginnings of the world we know now. In other words, those thoughts and desires within each of us about those who came before us and what they thought or seemed to value. Many would admit this is a common occurrence. That it is normal to have these kinds of interactions in our minds and dreams. What I would like to point out is that these are instances of our predecessors' values. In the event this interaction is in a dream it can seem a nightmare. Is it less real because you dreamt of it? Now suppose that same event happened while you are awake, but it seems only in your thoughts. Do you think this interaction is valid? Now consider these interactions were in conjunction with the end of days physically and spiritually. Again, I point out that what we consider reality consists of, and what someone from thousands of years ago would define as reality, are probably quite different. Our definitions may differ but the fact it exists is the value or feelings of the individual involved that determine the true scope. So, I will ask that you think about these thoughts for a minute while I deal with the next question for you.

The second coming of Jesus as we know him. It says he will appear with an army of the saints to retake or conquer the world and remove all of those who stand against him. How do you think this could be likely or possible to come about? Perhaps just like Herod did not understand the truth of the scriptures to pursue the discovery of who it really warned about.

Perhaps this time he won't have to develop the understanding or the faith to continue his pursuit of the truth. The world will automatically see his army and not gear up to resist with all the means available such as nuclear options. Maybe that is the slaughter it refers too. Or the rapture in which bodily people just disappear on a worldwide basis. Which do you think is more likely that God would do what he wants in such a manner different than he has ever accomplished his wishes and goals. I think that we need to see how our father has dealt with the ongoing disobedience of the children. Let's see one of the most documented was the destruction of Sodom and Gomorrah lets see the army he sent was two angels. He did it in secret without notification, except lot and his family. Yes, the inhabitants were destroyed but they had subjected themselves and their neighbors to the point of unspeakable acts occurred night and day yet did not raise an uproar. So, they were not exactly innocent observers. So, I guess you could consider that the removal of a fairly large portion of humanity. But I think it pales in comparison to the removal of half the planetary population. I know it is something he could certainly do if he chose too however, it would not be in keeping with the way he has dealt with us in the past. And as I have pointed out the purpose of creation that he as well as that which is his will get greater constantly. It would seem to me unlikely that he would choose to destroy the children arbitrarily. It is far more likely he would just allow them to continue to destroy themselves especially at the alarming rate of increase they have done since 1900. Consider the advance rate of the slaughter of his children since 1900. Over 100 million just to establish socialism in China and Russia. And that is outside the slaughter that occurred in both world wars. So, you see we have been anything but a threat to his continuation.

As you are seeing these things, I ask you to consider that the purpose of creation and nature itself is the constant growth and greatness of the creator of all the Alfa and the omega. Anything that works to reduce that is removed if not by any other means, then by nature preparing the same area to support more. It can be viewed in the pacific islands which started out as rocks, but nature turned into paradise at least till men got there to soak them in the blood of their brethren. It is this constant growth that is caused by a creator who loves his creation and encourages its growth in every aspect. For men it is especially important because we were given additional forms of energy that sets us apart from the rest of creation but still requires the growth the same as the rest of creation. I point out the possession of a certain kind of energy we would refer to as will. Because with it we have dominion of all around us. It is the way we have dominion, but it still must be in keeping with the overall purpose of creation. Obviously, there is much we do not know about creation but that is because we have sought to be apart from those around us. That is on a physical and spiritual plane. as well as the impact they have on the energy plane. So, if you have kept up with the story you know we are talking about the things that will happen and at this point ways that it could happen and yet be different than what society thinks will be. many today are looking for the return of Jesus, so they expect to hear it on the news, I guess. Just as Herod thought the messiah would come in a king's house. At any rate there are a lot of people expecting to hear that kingly announcement. The fact that God never does things the way we expect only moderately affects how they expect to be notified. Just this shows how much they depend on the thoughts and opinions of other's which should be in itself a red flag. Just because someone appears in the sky does not make them the Jesus so many claims to know. It is what comes from him that judges him not the thought that you give him. So, if you are to meet the real Jesus, he will talk of the same things he did the first time, which was not him but the father. Jesus never said pray to him he always said pray directly to the father if you are praying for the same things Jesus did then your petitions will be joint but if it is not praying for yourself for things he would not support will not be favored. He is for the will of the father not your will or as he showed in life not even his own will. At this point I propose that he is already here and working on accomplishing what he began. That would be making the individual aware of the reality of the gifts that the father gave to them, and how they have been giving those gifts away. It is when they understand that they will stop giving their power to others who seek the destruction and ruination of some of the children. It will be in a very unexpected and certainly surprising way. Because it is still what he said that contains the truth. It is something that will have to be reintroduced to the people since what they have been taught primarily is the words of what people said about how they interpreted the words he said meant. They thought it was the right thing even though they never considered it was not some people that the father made, but all people. It is easier to condemn others than to try to understand how the father worked in their lives to reinforce the truth. It has been the constant teaching that none are good enough and it is only through the acclamation of others that makes you acceptable. In spite of the fact that the one, so many claims to be a follower of stood firmly against that. He even showed them that they were wrong by removing what they were blindly afraid of. And he put that fear in the proper place which was the individual because they are the ones who can give them the second death. It is this renewal of his words that will cause the individuals to again serve the father no other men. When enough of the people reclaim their rightful place as children of the living God, they will remove the power men use against them, from the media to the people who have been given so much yet did not use it to enrich their brethren by rewarding only those who seek to better themselves. Many because they wanted to do something that would not increase their neighbors. If you do not stand for yourself, you will never stand in heaven. It is this realization that will remove the power of those who think they can wield it over you. This occurs by what many think of as the rapture. The thing many think of as the physical removal of the children of God who chose to work for and with him. In this many will no longer give power to others who seek to harm or not care about any portion of the fathers' children, no matter what name they know the father by. It is the creator of all that cannot fit in any name man can make because he cannot be limited or defined. It is this disengagement of people who seek to pursue something that will not improve the value of life for all that will make them seemingly disappear, because you cannot use their power against them. This is the rapture because without their power you have no power over them. Just as in the resurrection of Jesus the will of the father overrides all will. Which is why it is the fathers love for all he has created that will enable the dead to reassert themselves in this world in dreams or internally the individuals will have to deal with what makes them who they are scientifically we would say the DNA of the others that came before you. it is the nature of people to seek to try what they are told, to see if they can find someplace where it is untrue to them. If they can find a place where it is not true, they rebel against more.

It is one of the reasons today many thinks there is no God because he won't jump through hoops for them. But they don't think of it that way. They think it is scientifically inaccurate because they can't recreate it without considering that their method requires perfect recreation of everything that could affect the outcome. Even this is considered in creation; this may seem complicated but every part of anything must exist for anything to exist. That means the things we can see and those we can't have to, exist which requires all that is to be part of the whole and even though you may not like it or see it, it must be there for all to exist. As I mentioned consider the DNA that is in every cell of your body and consists of some portion of your forefathers DNA and consider the energy, they exerted during their lifetime to support or deny what they believed What that means is for life to exist that which is not life does too, because they define each other. That is the same if you consider good and evil. Good always leads to more evil is all of the parts of anything or object or concept but not the whole the things used separately which make up the good. Apart they are never the whole together they can lead to even greater, that's what good is. So, you see you can use evil to make good, but evil can never be good. That is the reason good will always prevail. It is the driving force of creation always more to the point the end and the beginning are one. Perhaps now you can see that even things you do not see have impact in your world. This will be true with those who have been before making themselves part of today as well. It is the will of the father and what he said will be, maybe just not in the way you expect or have been told it would happen. It may seem impossible because we don't like to admit that anything is possible.

What does all this mean consider the ramifications if we understand and refuse to be part of the use of our power to harm any of the children of God. We will unarm those who think they are above rebuke. I know you think I will wait till someone else does it publicly before I will do it. To that I can only warn you that you judge yourself by what you say and do. If you will not stand for what is right, you will not stand for yourself, and mankind will use that to keep you underfoot. So, you see everything that was foretold will not only happen it has to happen. Look at the world around you the insecurity the fear the continual destruction how long do you think that can go on? As

I have shown you there may be subtle variations in what I saw and what will be the reasons for it are before you now. The choice of how long you will wait is up to you. Understand that done properly there is minimal harm, but the longer people delay the stronger the hold those who seek evil will be.

It is now I can tell you what I hope you will see and know. The creation is powered by the individuals, but all the individuals are in the creator, and it will always serve to make him greater. Your division and demand that things be in the form you expect has never been the truth, yet you call the scriptures the living word of God. They are because they were to serve all the children of God not just the ones you think. So, as you seek things seek those things that will increase all, not divide or separate some. Jesus words are still true judge not lest you be judged. The words are as alive and truthful today as they were when people killed him for saying them. And the reaction to them is the same today because they see it as a threat to what they think is their power structure. So even today because you seek to be apart you will kill anyone saying those things. If an old man can see this, don't you think the father and creator of all will know it? So just as before he will remain hidden until the time is right, and the children have punished themselves and each other enough to change their ways. It may require that even more self-destructions occurs but that is up to us. Heaven requires that you are the individual, but you see all the other individuals just like you part of one larger individual and know if you harm them, you will harm yourself and that helping them will help yourself. Not because it is a rule but because it is an immutable fact. Heaven does not exist by rules it exists by love. I see that today many more will be troubled by the appearance of the values of those who came before both when they are awake and while they try to sleep. It is the promised coming and yet they will seek the answers of men hoping to find peace rather than face who and what they are, to know peace. Fortunately, this does not really take as long as the first part did. How will you know you made it? When you no longer seek to judge anything, others do but, try to find ways to increase each other despite your difference. Not only will you seek to increase them, but you will seek to stop others from judging them. Then it is the increase all will enjoy that is what heaven is and is for. You will realize that each are gifted in ways they can help all and because they have different tasks to perform their thinking and thought process will be different, but the fathers will and growth for all is the single most important factor. You notice I did not refer or inject money into this because it approximates what men to seek to control true value which is the feelings of the individual. Value is why you assign your feelings to anything and in heaven the most important is the father which is made up of all his children to harm them is to harm him and that means it will harm you. it also requires each to use their gifts to help themselves and each other. If you do not seek to do this, you will not be in heaven. Each has what they need, and their neighbors look after each other because they want to, not to determine what their neighbor should have, or that there is a police force that will get them if they don't. if they don't, they won't be there. So, you see the second coming will end in the eventual establishment of heaven here on earth. It is and always has been the truth and it has been inside us the entire time but because we thought apart from God instead of one with God, we could never establish it here. Perhaps now you can see how and why Jesus was the Messiah it is in the words he taught and message he gave, the fact that he gave his blood for the lusts of men was incidental. It would and very well may happen again because the Same prophecies that established the witness which was Jesus refers to two witnesses. And it seems there is no satiating the blood lust of men. And their desire for miracles to believe. It would as those scripture said be the same result, but it is horrible to think man's lust for what they think is power will tear the world apart. I wish we could be reasoned with without so much destruction but let the fathers will be done and woe unto the world for seeking to be apart from love.

You see everything the bible says will happen, will happen unfortunately for so many who think the name they give God is worth killing others for in spite of the fact that no name can truly contain him because when you name something you think you can define or limit it in leu of that we build religions around what we think we can define and control. Then we fight to the death not because we think God is right because we want to be right in naming something that cannot be named. That is why so many religions fail. That is why so many today think there is no God because if he existed it would be by our definition, which means vast amounts of people have died needlessly over a name. surely God would not want that. The fact that it is what men want to do that caused it does not enter the equation. Or the fact that God gave this to us and wants us to choose to increase the value for all. Does not enter our thinking. We would rather destroy each other than really understand that God does not need us to defend him he wants the best for us, however we must choose that. It is perhaps now that you will see the voracity of what the bloodlust was all along yet, still has been there and need for what we think of as supernatural continues. You demand that an army appears and forces you to love one another. Even though that would only continue the separation. Because all the ones that will be lost in that conflict would still be in the DNA of those left. You must be forced to make a decision to love stop thinking that force is love. It is this that has fueled the seemingly endless destruction of so many, this must be done in a way that was foretold and yet different than anything you could have perceived in your divided state in order to cause such a dramatic restructuring of how you understand power. There must be no doubt in the hearts and minds of the individual that will cling to them allowing that shadow of doubt that they will give a foothold to their fears. Heaven has no doubts, or insecurities. That is the surety of the [lace I spoke to you in my first book and has to be with you if you are to ever experience heaven.

CHAPTER 6

The End of Days

I have in this book and the previous book, "A place for you, the end of days." All the vision that I was given. It is what I was told to do in my vision, and it is finally done. it immediately gives me greater peace. In this chapter I will try to help you understand what this means to me, and I hope to many. I split it into two books because it seemed that the world needs the means to find that peace for themselves as quickly as possible. Like all things it is up to the individual to find what touches them. I am not trying to tell you what to believe.

I think that many who read this will think I am against churches or religion, I am not, I am against the partial truth, because it leads to the ultimate loss of value in one form or another. It is because limited is not the God and father I know. We are limited and we think in terms of limited and therefore most religions reflect the limited mindset of those who created and pursued that line of thought. Then they project it unto others. As in all things you have the right to accept or reject the limited understanding, it seems as though our rejection of something makes it go away, again our limited thinking. Jesus himself did not teach divided thought or action. Rather he thought the individuals need to control their own actions in order to reflect that which is good. Most religion teaches you are not good enough and that therefore the world will come to an end. Some final catastrophes that will end mankind. I do not believe the father would make that mistake. We are the children of his creation it is him who gets greater by our success as well as us. it is the nature all things were created for to get greater. Religions like weather are only part of the story. In one part it would seem to have total control yet in the long run it is to provide the further expansion of life. But as long as they do not advocate the harm of others it is the right the father gave them to choose for themselves. Even in the instance of disaster the remnants will go on, so these religions teach inevitably the continuation in some form of what they call heaven. The primary difference is that they say you must do what their limited minds say you must in order to be in heaven. If you understand the vision Jesus, had you are not separate from your creator and you have always been. It is not subject to the limitations of men. By his resurrection he proved it. We maintain you are never good enough and that nothing you do will ever be good enough to get into heaven, that is not what Jesus said, follow me be as I am. Which is going to be with and in my father. The concept of being good enough to other people is what kills most, the father created you even in your flawed state, why would he have done that if it were not possible for you to fulfill your goal? Again, the assertion of others to seek to control you. It is up to you to preserve the good for all and it is how you understand and do that which will judge you in both your fathers' eyes and your own eyes. It is how well you do that which will dictate the joy of living that you seek which is the only true value because it is yours to control. What I have tried to do in these books is to show you that you are not limited because your creator is not limited, and he loves you so much he created this place for you to make the mistakes that come with learning. As you grow so does, he. It is for this very reason that you must learn how to forgive yourself because your feelings can only truly be totally controlled by you. We use drugs which cause temporary alterations of our system, but it is still the individuals learning to control what they give power over themselves that will dictate long term growth and health. Part of the vision Was to see there are no ends and there is much more than our limited ability to see than we can imagine. I present to you this thought, some of the things we take for granted today were science fiction two hundred years ago transcontinental flights by hundreds, cross country road trips in days instead of weeks or months. This might show you that what you can imagine can be real but there are down sides to each as well. That is the part we don't want to consider but it must be accounted for every side must exist for something to exist. Our religions generally do not account for the other sides, therefore they can seem supernatural or dark because we don't understand, and they are not in keeping with what we understand as power. But I tell you the power that is used against you comes from you. This is critical understanding if you are to find that place I spoke about in my first book, it is the place which will give you the security and certainty that it cannot totally harm you. It is the place of peace no matter what is happening around or even to you. This is the place Jesus prepared and proved to you through his resurrection. We think of it as all things apart from us because we fail to understand and believe what he told us about being as he was in the father the father in us and one with the creator of all. It was not to make himself God over us it was to make the father one with us that is what he was sent here to tell us that is the message that made him the Messiah even though there had been many prophets before and since who had the vision, if they do not share and explain this vision for all not just who people select, they are not doing what he did. There are many men made religions including some that call themselves Christian, but if they do not allow everyone to be blessed when they celebrate God the father creator of all they represent just a portion of what exists and because they have limits so does their creation. Apart from each other you are limited in the amount of joy you can experience and as you eliminate each other you further limit the increase of joy that could have been, that joy is energy, the energy you were created to create it rewards all. It is the increase of energy we call mercy. If you throw it away, you eliminate your ability to do what you were created for. That is why one of the symptoms of illness physical or mental illness is the loss of energy. It is the reason we call depression what we do. If we raise the joy of living with and for each other the energy level increases as well. A simple example of what creation was for. And how nature was put in place to preserve the ability to increase the energy.

I hope by now you can see that in no situation others have ultimate power over you and that only you can allow others the power they have over you. If you understand please don't give things power over, you that do not lead to the greater joy of life for all. One of the assurances that you can have is knowing in spite of how you see things they are going exactly how they are supposed to, and that the only person you have control over is you. It is this realization that can give you the peace no matter what is going on to overcome. Everything is just part of the whole and the whole exists for the increase of all, and it will accomplish that. Even if you see the destruction of so many you do not individually have the power to change that but those who seek the proper goal which is the increase of all will eventually triumph. We each are only part of, but we are needed in order for the whole to do what it was designed to do. And it is not the judgement of the individuals but, how the individuals accomplish the goals of increasing the energy of all. This understanding is necessary in every part of your existence physically and spiritually. When you judge another, you condemn yourself. Remember it is what you seek that can happen not what you wished would happen without the attempt to make it happen. And you must recognize that in others as well otherwise you are just throwing value away. That is what you must guard against because the next thing is that people require without investment in success which will always lead to no success. So many think that investment is only money, but it is value that is require which has nothing to do with money. That is why so many things that we can't understand accomplish so much more than we could have imagined. Money is a tool but not the sole arbiter of value. I am hoping that I am serving God and his children by doing what he told me in my vision which is, tell them what you see, but I struggle to find the money to publish this second book and for that matter publicize it or the first book which I have gotten so many requests for money to get it in front of the people. But I know that this is what I was told to do so I will do what I can to get this out to who needs it.

I think so many think it would be so nice to have the vision, it is wonderful considering I need not worry about being in heaven because I know that I serve a father who created all things, and he gave me the opportunity to experience heaven and even told me I was always there even though I have not completed my task yet. It gives me hope that this task will be done. It may not be till long after I am dead, but it will help many. I pray that whoever reads these will be touched in such a good fashion that they will recommend it to all they know. I know the message since it was the same one Jesus gave is good and will always be. I am hoping now that in spite of the lack of money it will be done.

There are so many ways and situations that the understanding will help individuals, if for no other reason than to understand and forgive themselves. I had a traumatic brain injury seventeen years ago. It was disaster to the nice life I had going up till then. I lost most of the physical possessions and my income was cut by sixty percent. It appears it could not get any worse and I was only cognitively aware of part of it. I existed in what I call zombie land for several years till I had this vision. Even then I had learned to question every perception I had because so much made such little since. That comfortable feeling of knowing seemingly had disappeared. Even though I was only on a mild antidepressant drug and a high blood pressure drug and had been on them for several years by this point certainly no psychotic medication and it was in the afternoon. It was different than any dream I had ever experienced, when I was back fully aware of where I was and what I had seen I was in total awe. Remember I was someone who could not remember anything cognitive that happened the day before or for that matter the hour before I went to sleep, but this vision I could not forget. The fear of what I had been asked to do was for me very real. To begin with I had a brain injury why should anyone believe me, then there was the reality of what I was to tell that I know many more important people than me had been killed for and many times they were killed for things which were much more limited than what I had been told to tell. Then there was the fear I knew it was true, but I did not know if I could find enough of the right words to tell people accurately what I saw, and it wasn't just seeing it was feeling that conveyed much of the understanding. It had built up in me a resistance to even try to do this, but the feeling never went away, and the subsequent more cognizant visions seemed to continue. Especially as things in the world seemed to transpire. I got to the point I would not watch anything or listen to anything that would have the news on it. Still seemingly it raised and lowered with the concern of those I was in contact with. It may have been that my subconscious was far more informed than I was aware of, but it seemed like I was driven to the point where I finally despite my concerns felt that it was necessary to point out the place Jesus talked about. Remember my outside influence was extremely limited, and I had difficulty reading because of the ability for my eyes to track along a written line. I seemed to know these words as though I lived them, it was odd to have that certainty of knowing, back but only in things related to God. Everything else throughout the day was almost never remembered. As I said it was this feeling of urgency that I felt that made me more aware of my failure to do what I had been told to do, tell them what you see, then my fear was addressed in a way I could not ignore. I was shown that its not me but the father that really counts and everything has it's time and it was time. So, with my fears assuaged I tried to do the best I could to convey in the first book that place Jesus showed us through his life and the way he faced and then came back after his crucifixion the strength of faith and our father. The money was there to publish it, but I certainly had no idea of the number of marketing agencies that want their cut to present it to the people. It was published and available on Amazon of course without much fanfare since I could not afford it at the time. I am still not able to see how the reception is. But nevertheless, I wrote this book knowing there is a time and a place for all things I hoped to have the funds to publish and publicize both in the near future, but I have done what I was told to do tell them what you see. To other survivors of strokes or brain injury all I can hope is that the lessons here that there is more to your life than you can know but it is still yours to be accountable for you will be kinder to yourself and those caregivers and family members who are trying to walk with you through this. Remember what Jesus himself said and did "can the son of man forgive sin?" forgive yourself and all around you, you will feel better.

CHAPTER 7

Armagedon

Having had a traumatic brain injury in my fifties was like becoming a child again. My ability to remember anything was severely limited. My physical ability was also extremely limited not from mobility but from fatigue. What I found was that for at least six years I could function in a zombie like state I could perform most functions if instructed but struggled if they involved reasoning. Internally I felt alone and lost almost always. This extended to the point I was lost if I left the house even in my own neighborhood. Because of this loneliness I constantly sought to find out who I was because I knew I must have close family even though the chances were good I would not recognize them or remember them. It seemed even God was distant,then I was searching internally for him, I started reading for a few minutes each time in the bible hoping to find answers and I came across the scriptures about Jesus before the Sanhedrin in which they tried to trick him into naming God by some other name than they knew him hoping to say he did what he did in the name of Satan, he answered them very clearly he said puzzle, or answer this , I require mercy I do not require sacrifice if you knew the difference, you would know where my authority comes from. I think it was this state of almost childlike wonder that God used to take me on the spiritual journey. I asked God to show me the difference and that is when I was taken on this spiritual journey, and just as Jesus promised everything became clear to me. Because I did not have the limitations, of what we teach I really did not understand or think about what many would call preconceived notions about people or for that matter things. So, I would not remember long enough to be upset or dislike anyone. It was this state that prepared me to see so many things. We teach children division, and hate, we don't think of it in that way but that is what it is. We teach them their value lies in making other people want what they have. They can find things to play with. We teach them that those things are not desirable because they are so common anyone can pick them up, so they are not desirable. But the child doesn't know that until the adults teach it. They don't know racism or religion or classes until we teach them. That is the innocence Jesus was speaking of. As a man in my fifties, I got to experience that innocence. I will be the first to tell you it can lead to inappropriate comments and behavior because it is outside of the judged norm. but they do not truly fathom the difference until they are made to tow the approved line. We do this through isolation of those we judged inappropriate to play with. this system has operated and worked for thousands of years. However, after the injury I knew true isolation, and because of the promise of God I knew a true father I could rely on. Exclusively. Instinctively knew pain and would not want that for anyone and my actions and speech while socially inappropriate was never intended to harm, if it offended you sorry about that it is just the truth as I knew it. Not filtered through social acceptability. That is one of the reasons young people seek to shock the others and be different because they know the truth for them comes from within. Unfortunately, the point where others feel harmed or offended is so distorted by the relying on social acceptability it removes the intended lesson, and they eventually fall back in line in order to not experience the loneliness. The fact of the truth being beyond social approval and within the individual in nature does not stop people from exercising their judgement of one another. Children do not have this ingrained in them until we teach it. They know what they experience and learn from those around them and the world, because of this we teach fear, children do not normally have that until we teach them. The kingdom of heaven is without fear, and it is not subject to others judgement it is how everyone raises the joy and the value within themselves and one another, it is this that demonstrates true value not the money invested in things, the joy raised and shared they provide. So, you can teach your children they must seek toys that other people want, or you can let them raise the joy in each other by playing with what was free and provided for them. They do not ordinarily set out to hurt each other until we teach them that they must divide things from each other in order to raise the so-called value of them and us.

I would never recommend that someone experience a traumatic brain injury or a stroke but, what I would recommend is maintaining your wonder of childhood by allowing things to exhibit their true selves before you judge them. In fact, be as a child would be don't judge them just either play with them or get away from them. What I experienced as a result of the brain injury I am at once horrified and yet grateful for, because it helped me understand that being a child is not bad but an endless opportunity to see life from a different perspective. Although it may not be a socially preferred perspective. It is innocent. I must guard what I say most of the time not because I would want to harm or offend anyone but because they want social acceptance. It is something that I remember about Jesus saying it is not what enters you that corrupts you, it's what comes from you that corrupts you. If I slip up, I might say to a woman she has a nice butt but that was never intended as anything but a compliment. If she gets offended, I might have to say it's a shame it has consumed so much of who you are. It was never intended to offend but if they judge it so they will receive the feelings created by their judgement of it. I won't, that is never what I intended but they can take it how they want. That is not to say that you should purposely ignore social norms, it is only to say don't judge so quickly. What I discovered through this journey through time and dimensions is so innocent yet profound it opened so many understandings that to be honest I don't believe I would have even thought of.

I got to know our father in a way that is so different and intimate than I could have from the way we are taught to. I got to see things from such a totally different perspective. To begin with I have a hard time finding the

51

words to describe how you really are just energy but have form and see other things even though you perceive them as form they have no matter. The father himself is so vast that no form could contain him, yet you know unmistakably it is him. All energy is in him and comes from him so much and in so many different forms you can't find the words to define them. This he gave me so I could understand so much of what I was to see and experience. The heaven I was in had form and seemed normal to me, yet I know it could not be, yet I was seeing it and it was. Then when I wanted to be with the father, I was although as I said, I knew him but could not give or see a form. I could feel him throughout my whole being. It was like I myself was not contained in a form in him I could go anywhere. That is how I know I could go back to the beginning of all creation and understand the intent of it. And, that he is always getting greater. It is this which taught me the true meaning of good and the true meaning of evil. And why all must exist for any to exist. It is also the basis for the understanding that value comes from our feelings and that this was created to increase the value of all which causes what we experience as joy. It is this understanding that allows us to understand much of what we will experience. For instance, as I said the brain injury taught me loneliness in a form that is horrible. To be there yet unable to interact was surely hell. It taught me how we teach that hell is the result of what someone else judges for you. Having been there I know it is what we choose and make for ourselves by dividing ourselves form everything and everybody. It is to be isolated yet aware it is truly hell all of this in conjunction with the understanding true value comes from within the individual in our feelings, which we determine by what we choose to believe, can show the difference between sacrifice and mercy, it is not about material it is about feelings. Anything that leads to the loss of joy in our feelings is sacrifice, anything that intensifies and magnifies the joy in our feelings is mercy. All of this I was taught in an afternoon on a spiritual journey that I took from before time itself was created to divide and give us the opportunity to judge ourselves and either increase or isolate ourselves from the inevitable increase of our father. And by so doing cement our own hell. Not because it is what he wants but, because it is what we seek. All of this can explain why Jesus said seek and ye shall find, ask and it shall be given. Knock and the door will be open onto you. Because it is what you sought. We want to blame someone else. We want to say its others judgement of us that creates hell, in fact it is what we prepare for ourselves by eliminating the opportunity to share our joy with others that removes that joy. All of this and so much more simply by asking God to teach me the difference between sacrifice and mercy, still think it is so easy that it is inconsequential?

After seeing all of this and knowing these truths I was back here, still knowing what I saw and knowing it is not what people want. Obviously as I had even told the father himself when he told me to tell them what you saw, I knew that if I did, they would kill me just as they had every other messenger who had tried to tell this story. Still in me it remained, and I tried to make since of it all. Eventually as I watched what was happening in the world around me, I knew that even death was not such a threat as living knowing I was supposed to do something and not doing it. it took seven more years of almost total isolation, but I wrote of my books because I knew that there would be so many hurt by what I knew was coming that while I cannot provide the material comfort perhaps the spiritual comfort of knowing it eventually will be alright for them. So, I wrote about that place of security I had seen and knew was the place that Jesus knew of and prepared so they with their faith would be able to withstand any trials that were to come, even crucifixion. I know that it is up to each to decide what they will accept I just pray that this telling of what happened with me will give them the peace of knowing their faith is properly placed in the father of all. It is difficult to know and see all of this and still trying to function in a place such as the world has become today. But unlike so many who say they know the end is coming I can say the end of days as you know them, from your divided state is coming because you are orchestrating it in the leaders you select the values you serve and the failure to understand the love of our father. I can assure you it is not the end of time and those who seek heaven and love will go on Just as Jesus did and proved through his resurrection. As he said when they asked him how to pray, our father who art in heaven in no place did he say pray to me he did say be as I am. I have grown weary seeing how people harm each other and seek to be apart so sorry to see that and yet I know they will get what they seek. While I have seen and know the joy of heaven, I am in the hell that mankind makes for themselves but only for a short while and then I can go back to be with the father of all still praying that I will be a good and faithful servant and the child he wants me to be. I must admit I am looking forward to some playmates again that don't want to judge and who will raise the joy with each other always. If this means that this form is done, I am ready to move on. I just hope I will have been a good servant while I am here. If that offends anybody, I am sorry.

Heaven has always been with the individual you give it to others and so because you subject yourself to their judgement you may never see it. I have walked in heaven and know where it is therefore if you have not walked in heaven, you probably can't understand much of what I have said here expecting something that you cannot really conceive of to be real, but it is and always has been waiting for you to get past seeking to be apart from and choosing to be a part of heaven. So please forgive me if you do not see, but understand I only hope you will. The choice is now and always has been up to you. Since you do not teach or understand and continue to be socially determined then just like Sodom you will end up destroying yourselves with your greed. It is just a matter of time when you will achieve what you are seeking the destruction of others which will destroy you. I have written what I saw that day and have been blessed or cursed since seeing the world destroy each other. But knowing that which is coming will be so much greater than what you can imagine now. And hoping as many as have eyes to see and hearts that will seek will turn their backs on this separation and division and choose the joy that was truly intended. That the world may truly understand the difference between sacrifice and mercy before they sacrifice each other to society and those who teach separation.

I am the least of all who have been sent but the message remains the same. Surely as you do unto the least of these you do unto me. Join me in knowing that the least will be the all and the last shall be first.